Love

Forever

Poems to Open Your Heart
and
Free Your Emotions

By:

Wentworth Rollins

www.WentworthRollins.com

This book is a personal work of love, loss, and promise from the author's experiences tempered by imagination.

Published by: Groundhog New Media

ISBN: 978-0-9978801-2-0

Version 2019.06.21 Book design by Amit Dey

Table of Contents

Introduction

We all struggle at times to understand the great pleasures and problems, large and small, of life. If we let them, our emotional responses to these heights and depths can create opportunities for new insights and sensual recreation. At times, poetry can be the key that opens new emotional doors and walks with us as we go forward.

You can read a book and get lost in the story. As an author and lover of books, I certainly suggest doing that. However, if you can read a poem and get lost in yourself and eventually find the part of you ... you are searching for, I recommend you do that often. This collection of poems is here to provide a warm hand to hold as you move along your introspective journey.

The verses explore the greatest of our emotions, love, in its different dimensions and forms along with diversions into society's presumed norms, family and the honored place for pets in our lives. The words were crafted to generate thoughts and reflections, based on your own experiences. Hopefully each reader will be stimulated to foster new beneficial approaches to all of life's emotionally mixed aspects. As we each pass on our individual ways, we all deserve to clearly hear what our own hearts really have to say.

Please read on...with all the wishes and expectations I can send your direction,

Wentworth Rollins

BINDING DIFFERENCES

Junior lovers go together
Formulating a plan
Open hearts leap up at first
Before logic takes its stand

Waiting hosts the winding way
Toward that passionate day
Distant as it may seem to be
Demanding first, a fall to one knee

Unions, be they short or long
Ring out a beckoning song
Wave not this worthy endeavor
Trust first to ... always and forever

ONE TOO FEW

Oh, what did I do...
Or, what didn't... I do...
To live this life with...one too few

Oh, how can I truly know what I missed
And...just who I never really, really kissed
Where didn't I bravely or blindly go
What didn't I passionately seek to know

What didn't I do to be so missing you
Oh, will I end this life with...one too few

Oh, will this desperate feeling fade away
Will I accept life with one too few...someday
Or, must I eternally have one too few in life
And... painfully live with this endless strife

What didn't I do to be so missing you

Oh, why must I live life with...one too few

Will "one more" love soon come to stay

Or, will I miss her tomorrow this same way

Will it be one too few ... forever and a day

Or, should I still hope and hope and pray

Oh, what did I do

Or, what didn't ...I do

Too live this life with

One too few ...

Just ... one too few

One too few ...

MORNING COFFEE

So simple it is, and yet
Daily coffee for two
Early in bed, never to forget
Is the story for so very few

The cup that appears again at dawn
Lasts longer than whimsical wooing
Greeting gestures grow oh so strong
So, say it often by memorial doing

What we say with profound motion
Fills quickly our emotional ocean
Deeds struck silently are never gone
They sing their own enduring song

So start the day with coffee for two

Never turn away

A most special way to silently say

I do so ... Love You...

A sip ... two or three

And it's immediately known

Love is here to stay, in everyway

All done without words each day

DECIDE TO BE TRULY FREE

Oh to be...and be...and be truly free
Go from Janice Joplin to Linda Ronstat
Astound all around...ever time at bat

Work to find the golden key
Don't ever, ever just let it be
Stop the mind's black chitchat
Change life's binding format

Let love come with a dream spree
See clearly exactly what could be
With a foundational rounding sound
Let dancing music shake the ground

Hope hides under each fallen leaf
Beware that hesitance is a thief

So go for broke without despair
Seek your future with a personal flair

Go from Janice Joplin to Linda Ronstat
Astound all around...ever time at bat
Just be...for you...truly happy and free

Don't Confuse
Wishes with **Wants**
When you want a thing
You go out and get it.

When you merely wish
For something, you just
Wait for it to come.

— *JACK KLEIN*

CRACK THE WINDOW BLIND

Start the day with me
Please see exactly what I see
Look directly into the park
Don't wake in the gloomy dark

First the blind, then the door
That is how you find so much more
Walk straight to the warming sun
Just grapple on to find the fun

Dance down the wide open street
Lightly glide right over trembling feet
Let yourself be splendidly spellbound
Don't touch the rumbling ground

Open that blessed blind
And see what all you can find

RESADDLING

Completely alone
How can that be
Pricelessly not free

Inner reflections start
Seeking wisdom's distraction
Knowing not how...or when

Stereo scripts of yesterday
Resonate and scream
Look behind the dream

Slide sights forward
Look left and right
Beyond never's night

Foster first a limping run

Eyes now seek smiles to come

Together with the 'morrow

Soulful covers found at last

Smothered in a flowing wrap

Loosely fitted to ride again

WHY WINE?

Fill your mouth with texture

And your mind with hope

Select the wine of mastery

Fill life's broader scope

Work to live or live to work

A dilemma no more

Ponder, be not the jerk

Find passions wide open door

Varieties and flavors abound

Find daily actions that astound

Grill your earthiness out

Create an expanding pure route

Dance on every precious minute

Rock on everyday

Songs of love will find their way

Just when hope is all but gone

Push the glass to the skies

Wine first, all "no's" on hold

Live hellos, never goodbyes

Make memories to be told

WHY...NOT

Why think...
Risk not again
Better tomorrow
Maybe I'll stay

Why not say...
Wheels up to love
Fly with it soon
Flutter that wing

Why wait for...
Sweeping new ends
Halting retreats
Sprint right past go

Why not...

Let love begin

Go less the how

Narrow the fear

Forget why

Trust, love knows

WE...IS IT TO BE?

It was not you, it was me...
Blocked by the immaturity tree...
I was not ready or able to see...
What could eventually be...we

Now I ponder what could be...
But wonder again about me...
Will I hesitatingly wait...
And miss opening the gate...

By just letting the love flow...
I hope you will always know...
That as surely as time fades away...
This heart is learning how to stay...

Patience preserves me on the way...
Toward that sparkling someday...
When I will more clearly see...
The now hidden way toward...we

Don't know where or when...
But, should I find you again...
Don't let me think or say no...
Or ... even pause once, to go

HOPE

"There is no medicine like hope,
No incentive so great,
And no tonic so powerful
As the expectation of
Something better tomorrow."

— *O.S. MARDEN*

PICTURING

Portraits fall short
Of painting the plan
For work's filters in life's span

Happiness drives on
Fortifying emotion's stand
To spark loves' theatrical band

Friendship fills each life
Solidly driving the caravan
While holding all as Peter Pan

Circle back tears
Stretching, scaring and...than
All molds tight into life's plan

GLIDE ON

Problems may suggest taking the next train
And...that is not so easy to ever explain
Don't let it torment your selfish mind's reign
Beg off sadness and find the champagne

Float over the daily rapids without distain
Knowing that there is goodness in the main
Life may make the dark sky look like rain
When past the clouds craft ways to gain

Open minds soar with an airworthy plane
Just loose the knots that come from pain
Discover the joy in booting urges to abstain
Trotting down ground without constrain

Stay or go...do so, to your own lyrical refrain

Sing to yourself first to define your domain

Then cast about to fully engage your brain

But, before you go, know not to complain

Action less knowledge becomes a migraine

One recovery cannot hoped to maintain

So slide on the emotional ice in the fast lane

Dare now ... to direct your own campaign

WINE

Desert before wine...

Never, excitement to see

Clarity bottled as sentiments run

Champagne not rain...

Announces passions fresh points

Strengthening unpronounced fun

Winter's white season...

Riesling's vibrant tastes wave

Rays magnifying vast crystals of sun

Chill the glass first...

Weigh the bottle's remains

Filling life's measures is simply done

DIAMOND BRIGHT

Reflections become diamond bright
Prospecting for passion to softly amplify
Hoping to be polished in a true love's eye

That's the response we guardedly seek
Churning up thoughts once only weak

Flanked by history's shattered stories
Shake away all fainthearted worries
Mysteries abound as emotions break
Hoping to avoid any classic mistake

Dismiss bleak thoughts today as temporary
Love sparkles, when not tarnish with tarry
Restraint blinks out natures' fading outline
Look again in those eyes and all will be fine

RECURRING DREAMS

What if, where ... when in good time
Could something as simple as a rhyme
Help the little miss from a misty yesterday
Find new strength to look again my way

That almond mirror of such pure happiness
Sparks memories of forgotten tenderness
A creative creature breeds such restlessness
For a rescue kiss in this blinding wilderness

Is a simple long hug, too much to ask
Might the littlest twirls appear real at last
From a dancer so perfectly balanced afar
As we each peer out from a personal bell jar

Can a tortured path promise not to betray

Down what is unmistakably a muddy way

Find no clarity yet, as tested emotions stay

For, I know not how to fade them away

LOVE's LIFE GUARD

Are you saving me
Or am I saving you
Easy it can be to do

When love effortlessness works
With all the sensational perks
Whispering on the winding way

By defying all the chatty jerks
Managing those glowing fireworks
Ease open that stunning array

Bumps bind the passion network

Harder now to leave the fray

Easier it is for us to just stay

So we buoyantly swim along

Bobbing and stoking love's song

Easy it is to recue me and you

LOVE SINGS FOR YEARS

Devoted love, never, never to be undone
Intertwines the two, to surely become one

Untouched, the internal rite is so begun
Growing wide as the stream chooses to run

Deepening emotion roots and happily clings
To fluttering hearts on bright birded wings

A choir of smiles and glances perfectly sings
The melody strummed on gentle strings

So clear the sounds ring for all to hear
As love echoes on full, never to disappear

Blasting pure joy, blessing each perked ear

With harmonies composed, bringing a tear

So, hesitate not, act without fear

Love sings this song ... year after year

EVERYWHERE, EVERYTIME

Love freely...

Tempers not unanswered emotion

Reaching out with unlimited devotion

Love appears...

As vegetation surrounding a pure lake

And... embraces clearance of any mistake

Love stands alone...

Straining sand from passion's potions

Draining shores on troubled family oceans

Love alone...

Knows how honeyed sentiment grows

Removes cross words and spoken shadows

Love prompts...

Tolerant actions to keep lovers friends

Foundationally spun harmony to the end

FURRY TAILS

Rover teaches again
Learn now, if we can
Observe with insight
Routine wonderlands

Counting not trips
Confidence so clear
Certain each time
Floating tails near

Flying gray fur
Waving goodbye
Snaring not now
So ... spring full around

Spinning, ears perked

Eyes fluttering bright

Breathless thinking

Catching soon … Right

To our furry companions

It's just outcomes they see

Not failure or concern

How perfect to be

RHYTHM AND RYHME

Where did our special melody go
Rhythm, rhymes ...the tender words
Gone now for so long...that
All we catch are the distant birds

Why don't we know or faintly hear
The lyrical love song that,
Was too soon to silently disappear

Can we spin and seek to forget
Flushing out our imprinted regret
Fully paying the doubting debt
Starting anew, as if we just met

Singing new sounds less faint to hear

The lyrical love song that

May too soon again disappear

Coupling choruses can carol over the blues

Finding honey notes of affection to choose

Powered emotions bring a stronger beat

So, Lovers will not hear the sound of retreat

Singing new sounds not so faint to hear

The lyrical love song that

Might not now, so easily disappear

DRIFT UP

Young and free prompts feeling three
Spirits, moods, devotions go carefree

Let friction not tarnish the routines
Love painlessly polishes brilliant scenes

Tempt not to recapture missing love
Two hands in a loosely fitted glove

Live not in the wasted, difficult past
Find something warmly soft to grasp

History's shadows pulling faintly down
Records need not float sorrow around

No silent turns to jog or run away

Pivot toward the slightest excuse to stay

Silver dripping now again as before

Holds the treasured mercury once more

FAMILY THREE

Pa, Papa, and Tyke
What's not to purely like
As Generations rebound
Stretching life's solid sound

Teaching tasks quickly awake
Where, when never opaque
Responsibilities become clear
So, speak now without fear

Growing golden generations
Build essential caring nations
Singers live in loving tunes
Loosing tied belief balloons

Hug the shadiest oak tree

Foster family fancy free

Nurture loves miracle melt

You too, are positively felt

Papa, Pa and Tyke

Easily make life right

DID WE

Two manhattans ... maybe three
The night's wine begging a guarantee
Before I decide if I even want to know
Did I set you free ... or did you just go

What made you slip behind the moon
Was your heart off warmed by another sun
Did I miss catching your stretched hand
In some way you failed to understand

Did you drift off without a glancing turn
Because I forgot what I never could learn
Was this all ringing jingles in my mind
Did I just imagine us tenderly intertwined

Are you waiting, sipping one more rum

Thinking as I, there is more time to come

Lost in dancing, dreamy sweet analysis

Hiding hope behind worry-colored calculus

Will I catch a glistening glance from you

Can we blink back that moment that flew

Should we stretch and seek to now renew

Finding at last what we never fully knew

SHAROLIN

As life's many mysteries pass me I pray
I will always have this to say
Satisfied am I for I heard the Sharolin play

Alone I struggled to clear sorrow away
But ... continually did I have this to say
Satisfied am I for I heard the Sharolin play

Questions abounded on not trying to stay

Nothing know I...I have nothing to say

Was it enough to hear the Sharolin play

Devotion creates its own twirling ballet

So...it is really became quite easy to say

Satisfied am I for I heard the Sharolin play

Emotions silenced so as not to betray

And still... I have only this to say

Satisfied am I for I heard the Sharolin play

If I live not another single glorious day

I will always, always have this to say

Satisfied am I for I heard the Sharolin play

"We must all suffer
from one of two pains:
the pain of discipline or
the pain of regret.

The difference is
discipline weighs ounces
while regret weighs tons."

—JIM ROHN

CYCLES PLEASE

From lust, searching not for change
For passion slapping over the shores

Letting love's broad blanket float above
Toward tomorrow's endurable tolerance

Balanced back by logics strong stand
Up volumes exchange fixed bayonets

Striking often bared, tender emotions
Looking, longing for lust's hiatus to end

FINAL FALL

Balance drifting for a final fall
Forgetting most of all
Ever after obscures future's treasures
Muting control's momentary measures

Temptation's stinging strum prolongs
Singing seasons showery sweet songs
On open, wicked ears day and night
Fright foiled by mixed, brief delight

Wells of deceit too steep to climb
Seep into conversations every time
Regret's rogue apologizes struggle
Posted not off by words' candid juggle

Twice vibrates a non-forgiveness hum

Uncovered again, doubling the sum

Survival audibly kicks in

Tonguing once more strangling spin

OUR INSECURITY DANCE

Whispers floating on the gentlest wind
Waiting for the loving to gradually begin
Time for that warming, subtle glance
Before the opening body language advance

Many touching exchanges just happen so
Starting slow assuring time to truly know
Break not the pattern or hinder the glow
Hurry not ... Or you may be asked to go

Learning to array confirmations in the ballet
Assure growing tenderness in a special way
Always moving without tempered cache
That is how to declare you want to stay

Knowing that love's refuge is within reach

Cause us to knowingly move to the breech

With uncertainty that faithfulness will last

We seek to veil a cloudy, unwanted forecast

Blinded by emotion, logic still exits

The vacuum opens as thoughts persists

The gap only closes with loves strong hand

Unconditional commitment makes it expand

MANAGE MUST EMOTION

A tree hovers whispering so plainly obsessed
With winged emotion not finding any rest
Whispery seeking not to be depressed
As suns warm others so similarly stressed

Garrisoned only by terra's steady reach
Knowing not what's in the covered breech
And...far from once adoring couple's beach
Recovering little lost from vanished speech

Eyes flit, flutter to find the next somebody
Clearly knowing what is deemed shoddy
Caring less the choice becoming toddy
Trusting sober lights reveal nothing noddy

Unforgettable as the long, lost one may be
We must be just as strong as the rooted tree
Holding the pretense to be truly carefree
While moving on by penning a new marquis

New names appear to signal goodbye
That's what makes soulful history fly
New emotions suppress or openly magnify
The crosswinds of life not so easy to simplify

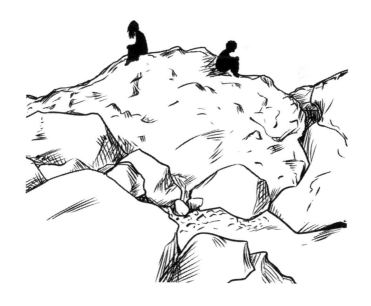

THE CHARITY WAY

Find signs of charity all around
Harmonic tones making a rebound
Life's rhythm demands a clear sound
To create open melodies to astound

Give we may and so often we will
Featuring life's best ways to thrill
Donate with kindness and sincere goodwill
For sham initiates will result in a cold chill

Differences show in each small soft tone
Instruments are many to be supplely blown
Each giving sound starts an echo cyclone
As we struggle unaided to not be alone

Food, money, love or a sweet smile

All giving is equal after awhile

For it is not the amount in exile

Attitudes alone cover that last mile

Play the petty games in a wary way

Not forgetting to plan for that day

When you will look back wanting to say

The Life I picked was the whole bouquet

THE RECIPE

Pleasure lives on every yearning street
As we wander along finding ways to meet
Chemicals precede the newly acquired heat
Culminating in loves special pulsing treat

Frustration comes from our lower shots
Excessive behaviors twist blackened knots
Nothing comes from wildly drawing lots
Cure the odds by connecting the right dots

No luggage belongs on this lofty air trip
Shade fears of losing both mind and grip
Healed and primed hearts ready to skip
Toward loves welcome warming pond dip

Promise not again the mistress today

Arrangements anew of frivolous play

Loneliness withers when the pattern begins

By finding less bedrooms to post such wins

Lust's vital role plays, but quickly departs

As intense emotions strengthens the charts

Advancing a moratorium on neoteric hearts

Clearing the track for love's flawless restarts

LIGHTLY SEEKING

Touch shines on a fragile glassed tear
Caressing so softly the oft tingling ear
Simply going beyond sensing what's right
Brightening love's art-filled, delicate light

Gardening about remembering so clear
Planting more seeds with no look to the rear
Screening the flow of emotions you know
Hoping to find new ways to completely let go

Few principles abound on which to adhere
New rivers swell as repeat bridges appear
Walk on the way with loves firming hand
Giving unconditionally is life's only demand

Mountainous beauty give nothing to fear
As we climb higher with less and less gear
Knowing what weighs more than it should
Gives relief to build-out all that's so good

Life's simple modes bring measures of cheer
Doing all while never being less than sincere

DO FOR OTHERS

Open the future for all good thinking men
Avoid being blinded time and again
Never to devolve into the comedian
Find ways to go from not now...to when

Brighten the light to fade the past away
Knowing that real patriots see a better way
To build a nation without trying to pretend
Learning hard ways to craft the right blend

Right is right and wrong is ... so, so wrong
Knowing good horses run the last furlong
Bridge the veracity gap, stay fully strong
Work hard to sing a crowd-satisfying song

Deepen the genuine search for good health

Knowing that is the measure of true wealth

Seek to honor this process without stealth

Conscious the effort benefits all in the broader Commonwealth

TRUE LOVE LEADS

Oh, so musical is true loving emotion
Coupled with commitment and devotion
Life plays out on utterly slow motion
Knowing love is deeper than the ocean

How do we create our personal story
Fancying out a hidden tender glory
That's so much more than the auditory
Never close to being toward transitory

Blend not the permanency of passion
Never, never reason toward ration
Love in not something to fashion
Go for it all and crammed compassion

Love does dies not of public exposure

It seeks the surety of gentle closure

Need it not the positive braced cozier

Worthy goes the climate of composure

Shadows loom as love lights the way

On the narrow path toward someday

Deny not what cannot ever be passé

Know, true love never leads you astray

EASE OPEN

Fall not, easing in and out of love
Removing fitted gloves that stick and tear
Open not emotions, packed so neatly away
Know for certain, slowing facilitates pain

Dig deep inside before the R 'n B stops
Thumping and making that perfect sound
Time strings on yielding dimming melodies
That stay within perked ears of yesterday

No easy modification could have made it last
Questions lay on airy songs now and forever
Hearing still the moving, distant refrain
As...Hope eases back in love's hugging game

Play small, be not afraid to risk again

Nothing unpins the past

Blot lightly as one new night makes two

Find stretched arms and whispers to grasp

Try not to capture what is now past gone

Differences touch, struck by a fresh dream

Stumble sideways inside loves shining eyes

Easy not, be present, staying until ... when

ASSEMBLE REGRETS

Concentration breaks, eyes drift high

Past the horizon's flickering elms

Emerald foliage's folds two hands

Hugging tender shifting glances

Nostalgia brings us springing back

Bridging emotional watery gaps

Sudden surfaces rock the scene

Mystically shaping foundational forms

Named stages push human boundaries

Master the man and machine mode

Seeking purer strength's silhouette

As, survival funnels past fault-filled folly

Embrace life's swelling, inspiring spheres

Channel tugs from aimless, roving targets

Know, focused connectivity opens roads

Bringing a personal "no real regrets" end

RIDE ON

Blanket, saddle comfortly know
Nuzzle, halter on, up we go
Horse and rider faithfully connect
Genes know what's deemed perfect

Cantering off the moving ground
Partnerships progressively astound
Bucking depression, flying free
Twins in true rhythmic harmony

Trust rectifies misplaced footing
Failing not, constantly rerouting
Flattening out travel's curviest risks
Calculating, so nothing is missed

Floating on toward greener fields
Trotting togetherness are the shields
Enhancing vital, indispensable senses
To clear would be hurdles and fences

The herd of two united so tight
Slice into day's glancing moonlight
For all who pedal to quickly foresee
No need ever for blending to three

SPIRIT CHARITY

Gifts honor the trembling past

Triggering the process to last

Big or small it matters not

Acting cleanses dusty thought

Happiness comes without prompts

Regardless of entangling swamps

Joys to count ride all around

Shouting a crystalline sound

Value defined by concentration

Arrives with deliberative causation

Minor inputs yield principal gain

Shunting those started in vain

Judge not the form or fact

Trust time and spirit to stack

The harvest seeded will come

Measuring to a glorious sum

Insure the continuing stream

Find life's blessed faith theme

Arrive through that open door

Deposit God's love and more

OUT THERE

In the fog with one less light

Searching for affection's road

Driving and driving and driving

Finding not love's lane home

Steadily going away

Fog and teary mist combine

Tracking and tracking and tracking

Redirecting the flow without a glint

Running from or to

Wondering why eyes see you not

Blinking and blinking and blinking

Grasping for feeling's stumbling sprint

River crossing come and go

Upstream with nowhere to float

Paddling and paddling and paddling

Mood paths diverge without gains

Numb the touches

Senses instinctively rebound

Feeling and feeling and feeling

Suspicions grow and pity reins

Summers shine again

Winter snows drift over the spirit

Waiting and waiting and waiting

For links to tighten resetting minds

FREELY SPEAK

Hysterical eyes in powered empty glasses
Punctuate each youth's mysterious plans
Knowing only later experience's messages
Governed not by risk's future cooling blasts

What good is freedom of every thought
When it's worthy not of critical capture
Die please, blessedly before futile analysis
Foster only reactive ricochets in voice

Stain not memories of the springing past
Tarnish less the fervent fast cheerleader
Hold for the zealous, colliding rebounder
Support fully spontaneous new reflections

Grab, use, expand, hold vital prime beliefs

Understand simplicity in complex thought

Push inspirations toward worded flows

Fear not...this crown continuously grows

"Nobody will believe
in you
unless you believe
in yourself."

—LIBERACE

FOCUS FRIENDS

Paying first the price
Makes no impression on the man
Patience upon patience upon patience
Revels not the images or the signs

Hobbled by history
Shuffling along, missing every bend
Wobbling and wobbling and wobbling
Time to lose the binding ends

Locate soon the walk
Twist not or stagger on alone
Searching and searching and searching
Find those missing dear friends

FINDING THE WORDS

Don't say no to shining your light

Don't say no to a hug good night

Don't say no to a dance in the park

Don't say no to kiss in the dark

Don't say no to smiles and laughter

Don't say no to plans forever after

Don't say no to a romp on the beach

Keep all your greatest hopes in reach

Don't say no to my tender touch

Don't tell me I love you too much

Don't say no to a quiet refrain

Don't say no to letting me remain

Don't say no to memories made

Don't say no to best plans laid

Don't say no to sparkling visions
Don't say no to delayed decisions

Don't say no to a new coupled presence
Don't say no to crossing this distance
Don't say no to love's sweet-sounding song
Find ... all the yes's that'll moves us along

REACT...AGAIN NOW

A beautifully bundled energy source
Appearing often as the darkest horse
A wine to be nurtured to full vintage
Opens hearts to love's bursting image

A kiss, a touch, a glimmering glance
Nothing really happens by chance
Meant to be...may not be
Without actions loosc and fickle free

Believe in love without any fear
Put life into a that fast forward gear
Never to be the same
Just, play life's most magnificent game

Once, twice, three time...never again

Step out and up or accept the pain

As, what could have been

Quickly becomes... never to be seen

Over thinking pulls the checkered past

Sparking feelings that should not last

Damping the runner's gain of ground

Precisely when love could be newly found

TOUCHING BEYOND

Tonight we reach the screaming sky
Daring not to seek reasons why
Again it is here
Accepted freely without phobic fear

Sketched portraits mingle together
Stroking the twin hero's brightest feather
Never thinking beyond
Staging love's precious positioned premier

Memories moistly mustered to mold
Find fresh feelings filled with gold
Posting first the smarter stake
Betting love's odds to safely break

Hold tight to the compassion cloverleaf

Capturing each joy benefits beyond belief

Apply these measures vigilantly

Hide in sight of senseless difficulty

Tolerance opens love's roadway

Past ponder some pushes

Harness passion power's foreplay

Solidify your logic-based sense to stay

SEASONS TO VENTURE

Summer winds whispering warmly in March
Bring back the season's light skyward push
As we pass again through the opening arch
With emotions sparked by a greening bush

Spring spirits flicker from flames never out
Fear of loss disappears into the shining sun
Love clasps the hands of two to shout
Never over think, find no reason to run

Fall and winter seem so very far away
Eyes brighten, shading perception of time
Knowing love will last past the counting day
As life's perfect duet still seek that rhyme

The fresh snow falls onto thinning hair lines
As icy cracks appear on each smiling face
Love's fireplace stokes mounting memories
To help each new night be shaped by grace

Seasons passing add fast blurring numbers
Wispy winters, serene springs and summers
None ever as joyful as the early curves of fall
As we picture nature illustrating a last call

So venture on down the next stormy street
There is someone very special there to meet
With seasons yet to come for both to share
Bringing lasting, loving joy beyond compare

PLEASE, AGAIN

Forever is just too long a time to be
Without you ... so I hope you now see
Why you never did fully appreciate
The many reasons to patiently wait

Commitment sooner .... than not
I know why this is what you sought
Eyes full of joy and worldly wonder
Ears closed to the coming thunder

Senses grounded in soaring flights
Forgetting splendid days and nights
Making thoughts jump to address
Your focus only on a certain ... yes

I wasn't there to hold you then … so,

Let's just forget I dropped that pen

And … create chapters forgetting when

We lost our connection without end

"Life is like an ever-shifting kaleidoscope. A slight change, and all patterns alter."

—SHARON SALZBERG

DIFFERENCES BEAT

I am following you again
Someday, don't know when
You'll let me take the lead
To dial a different speed

Pants or skirts never matter
Nor does the level of chatter
You burst open the door first
Not expecting to be reversed

The recurring question is...
As you foster a faster flow
Can I keep up this pace
Missing no turns in our race

FOREVER

Today I walk along dreaming
Thinking ... not yet, not now
Alone walking toward more air
Remembering...only "Forever"

So, pick me up, put me here
Place the light near me
Let me paint
Let me live, love..."Forever"

Must I post the loss
Scribe not until the morrow
The love now gone away
Reordered..."Forever"

The pace has passed me

The distance dims

Rewriting the story line

For today is the din of..."Forever"

Division dimensions doubt

From the silky syllabus of today

Toward the shades of tomorrow

The today, tomorrow of..."Forever"

Tomorrow looks in hoping

Hearing the trot of the drum

And...the laugh of the crowd

Singingly brawling..."Forever"

The society voice of ears

The society voice of ours

Cries to the walls

And drinks to the sky..."Forever"

Stock now

Double your step and ask

Who am I?

Forget and yet...Who am I?

I scream...Alone am I

Alone without my true love

Forgetting not

Living the answer ... "Forever"

There are spaces
between our fingers
so that
another person's fingers
can fill them in.

—*Unknown*

MUST IT BE THE SAME

We'll sing a song or two
And...play life's little game

When we are done and tired of it
Will it all be the same

Life's problems are too easy to see
As ticking torment blocks out glee

Somehow we never find the train
No matter how much the strain

So...who keeps things the same
Why opt first for filling shame

Must we miss the flowering fun
Every time we stretch to run

We trickle down life's twisted lane
Flopping with folly as dreams wain

Our minds held by an inner chain
As we seek new ways not to complain

So, cast your lot on the raging sea
Stream along looking for the key

Find dulled treasures in the debris
Never, never say ... it is not to be

Make regrets appear to be few

Gallantly accept some blame

Challenge all divergent drains

Walk away knowing you knew

Store nothing to later explain

Stand on each wondrous gain

Then sing a little song or two

Knowing...you won life's little game

"What you create with your own thoughts and emotions will be yours ... forever!"

—WENTWORTH ROLLINS

Acknowledgements:

In most every book, the author thanks individuals who were most instrumental in helping him or her develop and complete the book. There are many folks who have made such direct or indirect contributions in this collection of my reflections.

I would like to thank a young English major who motivated me to learn to write a long time ago. Also, I am constantly assisted from hearing different voices who encouraged me to do things "my way". There are many, many other people to thank who have helped me over my varied career. Those individuals, who are too many to count, each made a difference and thankfully stay in my ear. They taught me and many others how to get things done in the right way for the right reasons. This book reflects that benefits-oriented approach they shared toward broadening and deepening emotions.

My editor, whose soft, corrective touch always keeps me on track and my family who has supported me contributed immensely to the published result. What is presented in this book was learned from my wonderfully varied experiences. I will always be thankful for the up close view of love and life's great pleasures that were shared with me.

The graphic images throughout the book were provided for use under a license from Deposit-Photos.com. The front cover photo image was also licensed from DepositPhotos.com.

About the Poet

For further information or to contact the author regarding future works or a speaking engagement please visit:

www.WentworthRollins.com

or call the publisher's office directly at:
(814) 938-8170.

Hopes and dreams
Come and Go
With the Young
Never to Know

Wentworth Rollins, pictured here in 1968, is a poet who has wandered down the twisted lanes of love and life. His introspective, stinging, touching words bring you ... a unique blend of happiness, loss, splendor, strife and hope so you can:

Set your thoughts FREE to wander!

A Request

These poems were written to put voice to some thoughts and experiences to stimulate your thinking and emotions. If you found the benefits in such reflections, would you <u>please leave a review on Amazon</u> to help others know it is worthwhile for them to wander through these poems to accentuate their own experiences, gain from new thoughts, and release their warming imagination?